DO ASK, !

MW00677646

A ROMANTIC REVOLUTION

WORKBOOK

BY

CHRISTINA CHEMHURU (M.B.A.)

FORWARD

BY

DR. MYLES MUNROE

Do Ask Do Tell

The Romantic Revolution ~ Workbook
Published by Christina Chemhuru (MBA)
Copyright © 2015 by Christina Chemhuru (MBA)

P.O. Box 795732,
Dallas, Texas
75379, USA
www.doaskdotellbooks.com
http://twitter.com/DoAskDoTellBook.com
http://facebook.com/Krystyn777
www.christinachemhuru.com
ceo@christinachemhuru.com
To order go to https://www.createspace.com/4524357

Scripture quoted from the King James Version Bible
Printed in the United States of America
Library of Congress Cataloging-in-Publication data
Writer's Guild of America West
Chemhuru, Christina.
        Do Ask, Do Tell: The Romantic Revolution ~ Workbook.
        Includes index and forward
        Includes preface by Dr. Myles Munroe
        Cover image and design by Christina Chemhuru (MBA)
Title ID: 4524357
ISBN-13: 978-0-692-35146-8
ISBN-10: 0692351469

1. The main category of the book —Dating, relationship Another subject category —The Romantic Revolution 3. More categories —A Dating Guide Workbook. 4. And their modifiers.
I. Chemhuru, Christina. (MBA) II. Title. III. Subtitles
First Edition
14 13 12 11 10 / 10 9 8 7 6 5 4 3 2 1

Finally, brethren,

Whatsoever things are true,

Whatsoever things are honest,

Whatsoever things are just,

Whatsoever things are pure,

Whatsoever things are lovely,

Whatsoever things are of good

report;

If there be any virtue,

And if there be any praise,

Think on these things.

Philippians 4: 8 (KJV)

Do Ask, Do Tell

The Romantic Revolution Collection

Also by this Author

Do Ask, Do Tell Dating Guide

Do Ask, Do Tell Workbook

Do Ask, Do Tell Blog

Do Ask, Do Tell TV Show

Email:	admin@DoAskDoTellBooks.com
Website:	www.DoAskDoTellBooks.com
Twitter:	www.twitter.com/DoAskDoTellBook
Facebook:	www.facebook.com/DoAskDoTellBooks
Website:	www.ChristinaChemhuru.com

Books also available for sale on this Createspace link

www.createspace.com/4524357

Dedicated to the God whose faithfulness
has become my living testimony.
For more new beginnings than sunrises
I thank you Lord

~ * ~

In honor of the remarkable men in my life;

My Father ~ Jameson Chemhuru
My Mentor ~ Dr. Myles Munroe
My Pastor – Dr. Goodwill Shana
All the honorable men, brothers and friends whom
God has blessed me with

~ * ~

For embracing my vision, believing in me even when
you didn't understand me, thank you. May your
tears for me always and forever be for joy,
because, it's perfectly fine for men to cry.

Contents

Note from the Author

The Do Ask, Do Tell ~ The Romantic Revolution products are intended for a mature audience and as such the nature of the topics and the details contained in them are not all suitable for young persons. Parental guidance is advised.

This book and other products are written by a Christian woman but intended for a much wider audience not limited by race, religion, or any demographic factor that makes us beautifully unique.

There is no ridiculing, or gratuitous mentioning of sex, sexual activities, experiences, fantasies or sexual preferences in this book or any other products.

The Do Ask, Do Tell ~ The Romantic Revolution products serve as guides and tools. The nature of some of the questions will undoubtedly raise eyebrows. The elaboration of the rationale behind their inclusion should help guide you. Some actual experiences and findings in these sections will hopefully bring about some enlightenment.

May the results bring you greater joy, understanding, compassion, patience and healing so that you will learn to understand yourself from the past going onwards. I hope that you really come to terms with what you can handle and find it in you to grow beyond that. I pray that you will realize that the people you love may have endured more than you can presently handle in your life and that you are challenged to still love them. May this experience enable you to encourage others, and ultimately, may you finally let go of it and begin a new life together.

May *you* also forget… what lies behind - forgive yourself, learn to laugh at yourself and then invite us to join in the laughter. May you too press on! ☺

Forward by Dr. Myles Munroe

This erudite, eloquent, and immensely thought-provoking work gets to the heart of the deepest passions and aspirations of the human heart – have a good healthy and fulfilling relationship.

This is indispensable reading for anyone who wants to understand some of the principles of developing the foundations of good relationships in life. This is a profound authoritative work which spans the wisdom of the ages and yet breaks new ground in its approach and will possibly become a classic in this and the next generation.

This exceptional work by Christina is one of the most profound, practical, principle-centered approaches to the subject on relationships and dating I have read in a long time. The author's approach to this timely and critical issue of relationships brings a fresh breath of air that captivates the heart, engages the mind and inspires the spirit of the reader.

The author's ability to leap over complicated theological and metaphysical jargon and reduce complex theories to simple practical relationship principles that the least among us can understand is amazing.

This work will challenge the intellectual while embracing the laymen as it dismantles the mysterious of the soul search of mankind and delivers the profound in simplicity.
Christina's approach awakens in the reader the untapped inhibitors that retard our personal relationship, overcome our past hurts and develop wisdom for future success in relating to others. Christina's personal antidotes empower us to rise above these self-defeating, self-limiting factors to a life of exploits in spiritual and mental advancement.

The author also integrates into each chapter the time-tested precepts giving each principle a practical application to life making the entire process people-friendly.

Every sentence of this book is pregnant with wisdom and I enjoyed the mind-expanding experience of this exciting book. I admonish you to plunge into this ocean of knowledge and watch your life change for the better as you experience a future of success in your relationships.

Dr. Myles Munroe
BFM International
ITWLA
Nassau Bahamas

Preface

Dating is no longer what it used to be, from many perspectives. We live in a society that is immensely sexually charged. Where couples limit or completely forgo connecting on an intellectual and emotional level until they have managed to know each other in a physical or intimate way. Many place a much greater importance on exhausting their sexual curiosity about each other first.

The argument being, in most cases, that it is necessary to establish "sexual compatibility". So countless couples co-habit, engage or marry without knowing more than the template details of their partners' online profile. Yet they wonder why they cannot deal with discovering who the "real person" is that they are committed to. Then after the honeymoon is over they often accuse them of changing.

Often couples consider a series of fun-filled dates to the movies, romantic dinners, concerts, sports games and even religious gatherings as being the ultimate way to spend "quality time" with a loved one. Recreation in dating is essential, healthy and beneficial but exploring one's mate from a more intellectual and conversational angle would add more value to the relationship in both the short and long run.

So how could one get more acquainted with the person of their fancy where time may be limited and first impressions are often unreliable? Re-read their online profile? Stalk them? Peruse their resume? Run a background check? Ask around about them? Some of these could help but at best they would barely scratch the surface and at worst give a distorted image of the person being studied. So perhaps the best approach would be to begin to incorporate some pertinent questions into the conversation.

Of course one may have already employed this strategy several times from the initial meeting until this stage. Asking questions like, "What is your favorite color or food?" and "What is your dream vacation or holiday destination?" and "What do you like about your job?" Or simply, "tell me more about yourself". These are necessary ice-breakers for small talk but do not stop there.

Questions should be posed that can allow one to see their mate's life from a bird's eye view. There are those that help gain an understanding of one's history; the experiences that have defined them and influenced their principles and persuasions. Then there are questions that enable them to comfortably reveal their present state; their current mental, emotional, physical health and financial disposition. Not excluding their reflections on critical matters such as politics, marriage, divorce, monogamy, pre-marital sex and abortion, to mention a few.

Potential conflict areas may include religion, tithing, prayer and fasting, how to raise children, finances, pre-nuptial agreements, spending habits, debt and budgeting, and conflict resolution. These are just some of the areas that may need to be covered to establish the level of commonality or consensus already existing between couples. This will also help to discern which pivotal areas may affect the future of the relationship if disparity exists.

All these areas require effective tools that assist in exploring a person, their spouse/partner and the relationship at hand as well as in roughly predetermining, what a future with this person could entail.

This book does not attempt to or recommend psycho-analyzing a potential mate. Rather it gives the tools with which to help discover *together* who one's mate once was, who they are at present and who they are likely to become. Especially if one might have or would like to have the privilege of being a part of that transformation or their future.

This process does not remain one-sided though. It is hardly possible for the one seeking answers to not share and discover quite a bit about themselves too, during the same process.

For those who have already tied the knot and carried each other across the threshold, it would be strongly recommended to first read the entire dating guide first whilst making notes in this workbook. Then reflect on which areas are most pertinent to the health and survival of the marriage before raising them with the help of both Do Ask, Do Tell books.

One must determine how much they <u>need</u> to know and if they can handle the likely responses. Lack of preparation in addressing whatever issues may additionally arise may prove counter-effective. Poor planning may even result in detriment to not only the relationship, but to each other's self-esteem and each ones' ability to open up on future occasions.

Much care, caution and empathy must be applied especially when the information being shared is startling, shocking, disturbing or confusing.

Confidentiality must NEVER be breached even if the person sharing seems light-hearted about the information, or they volunteer it *seemingly* without reluctance. Sometimes humor or minimization are employed as a coping mechanism and should not be taken at face value.

Please note that when a person shares their personal information with another, usually a certain level of trust has already been developed in their relationship. Allow them therefore, to have the right and privilege to develop *that same level of trust* with the next person *they* choose to share their personal details with. Assume nothing. Ask for permission before divulging any information. As someone finally shares a burden that they have carried for what seems to be an eternity, the weight of confidentiality is shared. It is necessary to emphasize it so much, <u>be worthy of their trust.</u>

Be sympathetic and listen. Do not be judgmental. Suspend judgment for as long as possible and if you become uneasy with the information shared, discuss it. Pretending it does not affect you when it does creates undercurrents that eventually affect other areas of your relationship. Soon nuances and attitude problems will begin to seep dangerously into your relationship. Realize that the problem or challenge may not be so much **what** the other person had to reveal, but *your* difficulty in hearing or accepting it.

Do realize also that though this process could open up old wounds, it could also bring healing and closure to hurts that have been carried for a long time. Poor timing or insensitivity in dealing with the issues that arise could result in impeding the healing process, if not furthering the damage previously done.

Conducting these exercises well could result in immeasurable; increased trust, closeness, bonding and a greater understanding of each other. The shared experiences will help in being better prepared to love the "whole package" more freely. Couples could grow together in more compassionate and supportive ways. Even if the romantic relationship fails, a tremendous, lasting and loyal friendship would have been formed or re-created.

If some questions are awkward or embarrassing to ask and you fear being judged for raising them you can always use the excuse that "it was in the book!"

Remember, this is NOT the Great Inquisition. Create the right atmosphere first and try to avoid asking these questions over text messages or emails. One can be more reassuring in person.

Most of all, have fun!!!

How to Use This Workbook?

Use it to take note of what is of importance to you. Note **your** responses and those you would prefer to get or those you would prefer **not** to get. Use this workbook to digest past relationships and to get a better understanding of yourself. Use this to prepare yourself to answer some of these questions when they are finally posed to you.

Use this workbook to get more meaningful dates in before you commit physically or emotionally to someone. Get to know both you **and** them better and then use this workbook to have happy, healthy, fun and grown up conversations that will make you better partners and friends.

Use this workbook carefully. Don't leave it lying around without securing it. Avoid adding identifiers for the people you talk to so as to keep their information private. Develop a code name or nickname for each one if possible.

Try not to sabotage a good thing by being on the perpetual hunt for "red flags". We ALL have red flags! They are things other people ae cautious about based on their past experiences. So as much as you would not like to be seen in the eyes of someone from the past, give others a break too.

Finally, post some thrilling thoughts and discoveries on our blog.

Chapter One

What Lies in a Question?

For now, let's start with the touchy, feely stuff, which is not an easy area to explore for most but nonetheless an integral part of relationships. The questions in this section draw from chapter one in the dating guide where the foundation is already established. Work with both books to complete these exercises.

What Am I Feeling?

The following sections will help you tell apart your feelings for someone you are, or have been involved with and determine the intensity of these feelings.

Attraction

- People can be physically, mentally, spiritually, sexually, emotionally, professionally, financially, politically, powerfully, socially, or even vocally attractive.

  List **your** top five in order of greatest appeal. Beside your list, make another of the ones you wouldn't want your partner to loose. If you have other aspects you consider please include them in your list.

  _____

  _____

  _____

  _____

  _____

- If finding someone attractive is essential to your relationship, are you aware that any kind of attractiveness or appeal can change, indefinitely, at any time? What would that mean for your relationship?

_____

_____

_____

_____

_____

_____

_____

- In what ways do you consider yourself to be most attractive?

_____

_____

_____

_____

_____

- How important do you believe these aspects should be to your partner? If they place greater importance on them how will this affect you?

_____

_____

_____

_____

_____

Infatuation

- This emotion is often described as a passing fancy that is all consuming while it lasts. It can grow steadily without one knowing anything substantial about the other person or even knowing them personally. How do you identify infatuation?

_____

_____

_____

_____

_____

- What has been your experience with infatuation and how do you deal with it when you identify it?

_____

_____

_____

_____

_____

- Suppose one pursued a greater knowledge of both the good and bad of the person they are infatuated with, do you believe that a meaningful relationship could then develop, or should everything that follows be dismissed?

_____

_____

_____

_____

Gratitude

- Often mistaken for love, gratitude based romantic feelings are very common and similar to hero worship. In most cases, one may use one or more acts of kindness to project onto the person or gauge what their other qualities are likely to be. This often happens to but is not limited to parents, mentors, spouses, coaches, counselors and teachers. If you have ever been in such a situation explain what about this person made the greatest impression on you, or what had you done that impacted the other person that much?

  _____

  _____

  _____

  _____

  _____

- If you are prone to this emotion do you tend to amplify other peoples' good qualities whilst ignoring or excusing their bad? How did you become aware of what you were doing and how was it affected your relationship if at all?

  _____

  _____

  _____

  _____

  _____

  _____

- Have you been on the receiving end of this emotion and if so did this place undue pressure on the relationship and result in unrealistic expectations? How did you address this?

_____

_____

_____

_____

_____

_____

_____

_____

- Put unromantically, some have been known to consciously or unconsciously choose to love someone as fair exchange for what they have done for them or their loved ones. When would it seem reasonable or acceptable to love someone because you owe them?

_____

_____

_____

_____

_____

_____

_____

_____

Excitement

- Change is exciting. Relocating, a new job, new campus, being single again, joining dating communities, conferences, vacations, traveling, they all get us stirred up with the excitement of meeting friends, colleagues and even lovers. The mystery of the unknown has a certain appeal. Each time you see a certain person the thrill of anticipation could create excitement and yet dissipate when they are not near. This could become confusing because on one hand the emotion overwhelms you when they are in sight but you are almost indifferent or oblivious of their existence when they are absent. Describe your experiences with the romantic thrill of novelty?

_____

_____

_____

_____

_____

_____

_____

_____

_____

_____

_____

_____

Lust

- Sexual or physical attraction is the biggest reason people notice each other regardless of their gender. When the attraction is mutual things may progress to everything from one night stands, to lifelong commitments and the erotic nature of the relationship is sometimes the basis or even full extent of the relationship. Reflect on your past from this perspective and determine to what extent lust played a role at the beginning and throughout your relationships.

_____

_____

_____

_____

_____

_____

_____

- In your situations or relationships that were intensely sexual from the onset, did any meaningful relationship later develop? If so, what deliberate action or events brought this about?

_____

_____

_____

_____

_____

_____

_____

- To what extent did sex seem to be the solution to your fights or disagreements?

  _____

  _____

  _____

  _____

  _____

- Why do you believe these relationships ended?

  _____

  _____

  _____

  _____

  _____

- Should you or your partner suddenly or gradually lose their physical/sexual appeal how will that affect your relationship?

  _____

  _____

  _____

  _____

  _____

- Should you or your partner loose interest or the ability to engage in a sexual relationship how will that affect your relationship?

  _____

  _____

  _____

Sympathy

- From a definition standpoint it doesn't seem possible or even practical but sympathy is the reason many relationships ever began. It has encouraged both sexes to empathize with the heartbroken or lonely and feel that if they were in their position they too would like a particular person to believe that they deserved their love. From teenage crushes to present day relationships, family and friends have seen what we may not have seen in someone who vied and longed for our attention. Saying, "After all, they can't be so bad", "Look how their ex treated them, they deserve better", "just give 'em a chance", "Poor thing... widowed/ divorced/single parent and still they believe in love". Describe the occasions that these arguments have been made to you for someone, or you even made them for someone you thought deserved your affection and behold a relationship started.

_____

_____

_____

_____

_____

_____

_____

_____

_____

- If a relationship did ensue, what other factors, if any, motivated you to give it a chance?

  _____

  _____

  _____

  _____

- When their situation changed or the reason you felt sympathy for them no longer existed, how did that affect the relationship?

  _____

  _____

  _____

  _____

- Looking back now are you still moved with sympathy or inclined to love them? Why, or why not?

  _____

  _____

  _____

  _____

  _____

- How will this affect your future decisions to give someone a chance because of their present situation or persistence?

  _____

  _____

  _____

Love

- How do you define love?

  _____

  _____

  _____

  _____

  _____

- Do you believe in love at first sight, falling in love or growing to love or any of the above? Please explain.

  _____

  _____

  _____

  _____

  _____

  _____

- If you have ever been in love, how did you know it was love?

  _____

  _____

  _____

  _____

  _____

- In the instances when you were sure you were in love what did you know to be good about the other person?

  _____

  _____

  _____

- What did you know to be bad about the other person?

_____

_____

_____

_____

_____

- What trials and tests do you believe your love survived and therefore proved it to be real, if any?

_____

_____

_____

_____

_____

- What things do you think could cause you to stop loving someone?

_____

_____

_____

_____

_____

- If you thought this book might raise those issues would you stop reading or doing these exercises with your partner now? If so, why?

_____

_____

_____

If you are convinced that a stronger and more meaningful relationship can only be built by gaining a better understanding of each other and yourself, then read on. If you desire to be ready for a lasting relationship built upon a strong friendship with someone now or in the future then you will need to ask yourself some serious questions.

1. Do the feelings I have or the present nature of the relationship necessitate getting to know the other person better?

_____

_____

_____

_____

_____

_____

2. If applicable, does the other person feel the same way?

_____

_____

_____

_____

_____

3. Do I think I can be or should be trusted with their answers? Why?

_____

_____

_____

_____

_____

_____

4. Can I be trusted with the truthful response - that I won't use it against this person to violate their trust or hurt them?

    _____

    _____

    _____

    _____

    _____

5. Can I handle the expected and unexpected responses that I may get?

    _____

    _____

    _____

    _____

    _____

6. What if I get what I consider to be a "wrong" or undesirable answer?

    _____

    _____

    _____

    _____

    _____

7. Should either of us become angry or upset what should we do next?

    _____

    _____

    _____

8. In the event that either of us suddenly feels cheated or guilty, how will we get past this? What will our next steps be?

_____

_____

_____

_____

_____

9. Should the other person disclose criminal or illegal activities in their past, what should we do?

_____

_____

_____

_____

_____

10. Am I prepared to keep this relationship going if I get answers I am not ready or willing to deal with?

_____

_____

_____

_____

_____

11. What are my reasons for needing to know this person much better?

_____

_____

_____

12. Am I able to and ready to respect the answer I receive and treat it with the gravity and confidentiality it deserves?

_____

_____

_____

_____

_____

13. If I don't believe the answer to be the truth, should I pursue the truth?

_____

_____

_____

_____

_____

14. If I cannot readily get an answer – is delay tantamount to denial/refusal?

_____

_____

_____

_____

_____

15. If an answer or explanation is completely denied or the other person closes up, what will that mean for us?

_____

_____

_____

16. If either of us believes certain things should remain secrets for the health of the relationship, should that be a decision for one person alone?

_____

_____

_____

_____

17. What if the other person believes in full disclosure, does that mean I can never keep certain things to myself, even things told to me in confidence? How will I protect certain details without a backlash?

_____

_____

_____

_____

18. Should we set boundaries before we start and revisit them when ready?

_____

_____

_____

_____

_____

19. Will this answer in 18. Help me make participate more freely? If so why?

_____

_____

_____

20. Is there a better or "best time" to ask this question, if so, can it wait?

_____

_____

_____

_____

_____

21. How will I decide if I really <u>need</u> clarity or if I am just curious?

_____

_____

_____

_____

_____

22. In certain instances, when asked the same or a similar question would I be able to answer it comfortably?

_____

_____

_____

_____

_____

23. What if I am unable or unwilling to answer the same question, should I still ask it if it's important to me? How will I justify that?

_____

_____

_____

_____

24. If the same question offends or upsets me can I ask it but refuse to answer it when asked? If the tables were turned would I complain?

_____

_____

_____

_____

_____

25. What if I don't know how to interpret the answer, can I ask a third party or will that be a violation of this person's confidence in me?

_____

_____

_____

_____

_____

_____

Chapter Two

Ice-Breaker Questions

Use the corresponding chapter in the Do Ask Do tell Dating Guide to lay the foundation before you both begin to work through this chapter.

26. What did you dream of becoming when you were a child?

_____

_____

_____

_____

27. What jobs have you had and what is your present occupation?

_____

_____

_____

_____

28. If you did not need to work for money, what would you do and why?

_____

_____

_____

_____

29. Which was your best job ever and why?

_____

_____

_____

_____

30. Which was your worst job ever and why?

_____

_____

_____

31. If you were an animal, which animal would you be and why?

_____

_____

32. If you were an animal of the opposite gender, if different, which animal would you be and why?

_____

_____

33. If you were a bird, which bird would you be and why?

_____

_____

_____

34. If you were a bird of the opposite gender, if different, which bird would you be and why?

_____

_____

_____

35. If you <u>had</u> to be any other person on earth (dead/alive) who would it be and why?

_____

_____

_____

_____

36. If you <u>had</u> to be any other person on earth, of the opposite gender (dead/alive) who would it be and why?

_____

_____

_____

_____

37. Do you consider yourself as ambitious? Please explain.

_____

_____

_____

_____

38. If your childhood dream changed what dream/s that took its place?

_____

_____

_____

_____

39. Do you consider yourself to be accomplished? Why or why not?

_____

_____

_____

_____

_____

_____

_____

_____

40. On a lighter note, do you dream in color, black and white, hues of blue, green, brown etc.? Describe some dreams and the vivid colors you remember.

_____

_____

_____

_____

_____

_____

_____

_____

_____

Chapter Three

Deal Breakers

41. You have just started seeing someone, or you have been dating for a while, what things about them would be deal breakers for you?

_____

_____

_____

_____

_____

42. Why would you see these as deal breakers or seriously consider ending the relationship over them?

_____

_____

_____

_____

_____

43. You have been steadily or seriously dating someone, and may have made some commitments to them as far as your relationship is concerned. What things would be deal breakers if you found them out at this stage?

_____

_____

_____

_____

_____

_____

44. Why would you see these as deal breakers or seriously consider ending the relationship over them?

_____

_____

_____

_____

_____

45. Ask the other person in the following manner.

Have you ever been hit by a "woman"? (if you are asking a man) or, Have you ever hit a "man"? (if you are asking a woman)

_____

_____

46. What had happened? Narrate the whole incident including how it ended.

_____

_____

_____

_____

_____

_____

47. Now ask the other person in this manner.

Have you ever hit a "woman"? (if you are asking a man) or,

Have you ever been hit *by* a "man"? (if you are asking a woman)

_____

_____

_____

48. What had happened? Narrate the whole incident including how it ended.

_____

_____

_____

_____

_____

_____

49. If you or anyone has ever observed a pattern, how or why do you believe most of your relationships start?

_____

_____

_____

_____

_____

50. If there is a perceived similarity to how or why some of them have ended please explain

_____

_____

_____

_____

_____

_____

51. Do you still maintain good relationships with any of your exes? Explain.

_____

_____

_____

_____

52. Are you currently involved with, still in love with or have lingering feelings for someone from a previous relationship? Please explain

_____

_____

_____

_____

_____

_____

_____

_____

_____

53. Are you interested in or not interested in a monogamous relationship at this stage? Please give reasons for your answer.

_____

_____

_____

_____

_____

54. At which point do you think a dating couple should become exclusive?

_____

_____

_____

_____

_____

55. Were/are any of your exes problematic? Please explain.

_____

_____

_____

_____

_____

56. Have you or your family members or friends ever had to call the police, file charges or obtain a restraining order on any of your previous partners? This is regardless of whether the matter was later dropped, or solved between the two of you. Describe the events that led to this.

_____

_____

_____

_____

_____

_____

_____

_____

57. Have any of your previous partners or their family ever had to call the police, file charges or obtain a restraining order on you whether the matter was later dropped, or solved between the two of you? Explain.

_____

_____

_____

_____

_____

_____

_____

58. What is your position on each of the following issues? Provide examples where possible to better explain your preference or position.

    a.   Current marital status whilst dating

        _____

        _____

        _____

        _____

        _____

    b. Cheating

        _____

        _____

        _____

        _____

        _____

c. Monogamy

_____
_____
_____
_____
_____
_____

d. Marriage

_____
_____
_____
_____
_____
_____

e. Co-habitation

_____
_____
_____
_____
_____
_____

f. Divorce

_____
_____
_____
_____

g. Social lifestyle

_____

_____

_____

_____

_____

_____

h. Disclosing one's sexual history and current lifestyle

_____

_____

_____

_____

_____

_____

_____

i. Children

_____

_____

_____

_____

_____

_____

_____

j. Dependents – family members

_____

_____

_____

_____

_____

_____

_____

_____

k. Disclosing ones family medical and mental health history

_____

_____

_____

_____

_____

_____

_____

l. Physical fitness/attractiveness

_____

_____

_____

_____

_____

m. Dietary habits

_____

_____

_____

_____

_____

_____

_____

n. Past and current addictions

_____

_____

_____

_____

_____

_____

_____

o. Past and current use of drugs, alcohol and tobacco

_____

_____

_____

_____

_____

_____

_____

_____

p. Gambling

_____

_____

_____

_____

_____

_____

_____

_____

q. Financial stability/savings

_____

_____

_____

_____

_____

_____

_____

_____

r. Debt, credit cards and loans

_____

_____

_____

_____

_____

_____

_____

s. Credit score

_____

_____

_____

_____

_____

_____

_____

t. Pre-nuptial agreements

_____

_____

_____

_____

_____

_____

u. Divorce

_____

_____

_____

_____

_____

_____

_____

v. Job stability

_____

_____

_____

_____

_____

_____

_____

w. Education level/background

_____

_____

_____

_____

_____

_____

x. Criminal records and history

_____

_____

_____

_____

_____

_____

_____

_____

y. Cleanliness and domestication

_____

_____

_____

_____

_____

_____

_____

z. Personal hygiene

_____

_____

_____

_____

_____

_____

_____

_____

_____

The topics listed above can be both deal-breakers as well as pet peeves. Being upfront as this stage can let the other person know if a relationship would or not succeed if before too much is invested. It would be very beneficial to cover these questions over the initial meetings or dates and certainly before being intimate with each other. It would make walking away or deciding to be just friends much easier and safer.

Chapter Four

You - The Real You

59. What is your personal philosophy on life, if you have one?

_____

_____

_____

_____

_____

_____

_____

60. What is your life's purpose as you best understand it at this stage?

_____

_____

_____

_____

_____

_____

61. How would you best describe yourself?

_____

_____

_____

_____

_____

_____

62. How would your friends describe you?

_____

_____

_____

_____

_____

63. How would your family describe you?

_____

_____

_____

_____

64. How would your previous romantic partners/exes describe you?

_____

_____

_____

_____

_____

65. Describe what you believe are your best or finer qualities

_____

_____

_____

_____

_____

66. What are your life's greatest achievements?

_____

_____

_____

_____

67. Which are you not so proud about and how have you tried to change it?

_____

_____

_____

_____

_____

_____

68. What aggravates you or makes you angry?

_____

_____

_____

_____

_____

69. What do you say or do when you get really angry or frustrated?

_____

_____

_____

_____

_____

_____

70. Describe the instances when you have had to regret your actions from when you were angry?

_____

_____

_____

_____

_____

_____

71. How challenging do you find it to forgive people? Provide examples.

_____

_____

_____

_____

_____

_____

72. Which words or what actions do you consider to be unforgivable?

_____

_____

_____

_____

_____

_____

_____

73. Describe a time when you were determined to, and successfully paid back someone for having wronged you. Did you ever regret doing so?

_____

_____

_____

_____

_____

_____

_____

74. How easily do you get along with all/most of your family members?

_____

_____

_____

_____

_____

75. Do you have any enemies? Explain how you think they came about.

_____

_____

_____

_____

_____

_____

76. Describe situations in which you feel most vulnerable or afraid?

_____

_____

_____

_____

_____

_____

_____

77. In which moments in life do you tend to feel lonely? What do you do?

_____

_____

_____

_____

78. How do you handle loneliness when single? Does it prompt you to date?

_____

_____

_____

_____

_____

_____

_____

_____

79. How easy do you find it to make new friends? Describe your behavior at an airport, conference, church, or any place with lots of strangers.

_____

_____

_____

_____

_____

_____

80. How easy do you find it easy to trust people? What safeguards do you employ?

_____

_____

_____

_____

_____

_____

81. If you have any close friends describe how long and how well you have known each other and the most unique thing about your friendship.

_____

_____

_____

_____

_____

_____

82. How would your best friend/s describe you?

_____

_____

_____

_____

_____

_____

_____

83. How might this be different from how your family members describe you?

_____

_____

_____

_____

_____

_____

84. To what extent does your family and friends' approval/opinion of your partner or date affect your choice to commit to them?

_____

_____

_____

_____

_____

_____

85. Has this always been the case? Please explain your answer.

_____

_____

_____

_____

_____

_____

_____

_____

_____

_____

_____

86. If you have any extreme qualities to your personality that you are either personally aware of or have been told of by others please describe them

_____

_____

_____

_____

_____

_____

_____

_____

_____

Chapter Five

Childhood and Children

Formative Relationships

87. Who was primarily responsible for the household that you were raised in? Describe your household lifestyle as you can best remember it.

_____

_____

_____

_____

_____

_____

_____

88. If you were raised in a single parent household, describe your lifestyle and the things that impacted you most.

_____

_____

_____

_____

_____

_____

_____

_____

89. Describe your parent/s' educational/training or work backgrounds?

_____

_____

_____

_____

_____

_____

90. What were their sources of income? What do they presently do?

_____

_____

_____

_____

91. Have you ever been exposed to relationships where the woman earned a higher income than the man or the man stayed at home or was unemployed and the woman went to work? If so, what did you observe or appreciate from their roles and how the couple embraced them?

_____

_____

_____

_____

_____

_____

_____

92. If you have been in a situation where you were financially dependent on your mate describe how the situation came about and how you both handled your roles. For example, did you discuss and define them?

_____

_____

_____

_____

_____

_____

_____

_____

93. If you were to find yourself in a situation where you would be financially dependent on your mate for any period of time, how do you see yourself handling it? If unexpected how do you think they would handle it?

_____

_____

_____

_____

_____

_____

_____

_____

94. How many siblings do you have and what are their present occupations?

_____

_____

_____

_____

_____

_____

_____

_____

95. Describe your past and present relationship with your parents.

_____

_____

_____

_____

_____

_____

96. Describe your past and current relations with your each of your siblings?

_____

_____

_____

_____

97. How are your siblings' romantic relationships and/marriages?

_____

_____

_____

_____

_____

_____

_____

98. Describe any concerns you or other family members have had about any of these relationships including yours.

_____

_____

_____

_____

_____

_____

_____

99. Taking a step back, how do you feel your parents' relationships have impacted you and your siblings' relationships?

_____

_____

_____

_____

_____

_____

_____

100. Thinking back, what resolutions did you make when you pictured yourself as someone's' spouse based on all this?

_____

_____

_____

_____

_____

_____

_____

101. Do your siblings have children or desire to have any children? How has this affected you?

_____

_____

_____

_____

_____

102. Do you desire to have children, if so, how many and how near or far into the future? If not why not?

_____

_____

_____

_____

_____

_____

_____

_____

Discipline, Punishment & Parenting Styles

103. Describe your childhood?

_____

_____

_____

_____

_____

_____

_____

_____

_____

104. What were your most memorable moments from your childhood?

_____

_____

_____

_____

_____

_____

105. Which do recall were your worst or most unpleasant experiences?

_____

_____

_____

_____

_____

_____

_____

106. Describe any experiences that you recall as being abusive

_____

_____

_____

_____

_____

_____

107. Where you ever bullied, and if so, by whom and how did you handle it?

_____

_____

_____

_____

_____

_____

_____

_____

108. Did you ever get into trouble at school? If so, what had happened?

_____

_____

_____

_____

_____

_____

109. Did you ever get into trouble at home? If so, what had happened?

_____

_____

_____

_____

_____

_____

_____

110. Describe how you were punished and rewarded as a child and how you feel about that now?

_____

_____

_____

_____

_____

_____

_____

111. If you ever received corporal punishment in the form of caning, whipping or belting etc., please explain who punished you and on what occasions.

_____

_____

_____

_____

_____

_____

112. How have you resolved, managed or coped with any negative childhood experiences?

_____

_____

_____

_____

_____

113. How did you identify the issues that still needed to be resolved?

_____

_____

_____

_____

_____

114. Whom did you address these experiences? With your parents, pastor, counselor, relatives, spouse/partner, sibling/s or someone else?

_____

_____

_____

_____

115. If so, what was their reaction and did you feel it was helpful? Explain.

_____

_____

_____

_____

116. How did you respond/relate to persons in positions of authority when you were growing up?

_____

_____

_____

_____

_____

_____

117. What resolutions did you make or have you made when you picture yourself as a parent based on your past role models?

_____

_____

_____

_____

_____

_____

118. As a parent/potential parent do you feel you have managed to correct or will be able to correct what errors you believe your parents made if any? What will you do differently and how do you propose to do that?

_____

_____

_____

_____

_____

_____

New Beginnings

119. If you are a parent/guardian or have frequent occasions to deal with minors, how do you feel about the way you relate with children?

_____

_____

_____

_____

_____

_____

120. Describe your relationship with the other parent/s of your children if applicable.

_____

_____

_____

_____

_____

121. How do your parenting styles differ?

_____

_____

_____

_____

_____

_____

122. What is, or what would be your approach to disciplining children?

_____

_____

_____

_____

_____

_____

123. What methods of punishment do/would you prefer for your children?

_____

_____

_____

_____

_____

_____

_____

124. If corporal punishment is one of them, please explain how you would administer it, on what occasions and until what age.

_____

_____

_____

_____

_____

_____

_____

_____

125. How involved would you like your new spouse or partner to be, or what role would you like them to have in raising, disciplining and mentoring your children?

_____

_____

_____

_____

_____

_____

_____

_____

126. Describe your position on raising your children in a religious/ non-religious home.

_____

_____

_____

_____

_____

_____

_____

_____

_____

_____

127. Would you consider starting a new family with someone? Explain.

_____

_____

_____

_____

_____

_____

128. What would you say or do if a new or potential spouse/partner desired to start a family soon or right away?

_____

_____

_____

_____

_____

_____

_____

129. What would you say/do if a new or potential spouse/partner did not want to start a family soon or right away?

_____

_____

_____

_____

_____

_____

_____

_____

130. If you both desired to start a family and either you or your partner was unable to have children how would this affect your decision to stay in the relationship with them?

_____

_____

_____

_____

_____

131. Would adoption be an option you would be willing to consider?

_____

_____

_____

_____

_____

132. If it is possible that you or your partners' culture, upbringing or belief system encourages you to live with or have financial responsibility of your parents, siblings or any relatives do you feel you have sufficiently discussed and disclosed this with each other? If not, why not?

_____

_____

_____

_____

_____

133. Discuss any strong cultural background that you would like to incorporate when raising your children. How would resistance from your partner affect you?

_____

_____

_____

_____

_____

_____

_____

_____

134. If your partner had a preference to raise their children according to their culture, would you agree and if not, what would you resolve to do?

_____

_____

_____

_____

_____

_____

_____

_____

_____

135. How involved would you like either of your families to be in raising your children? What if they expected to, how would you handle this and how would you handle their desire to not be involved?

_____

_____

_____

_____

_____

_____

_____

_____

136. What are the no-compromise issues regarding your preferred parenting style? Explain why you feel so strongly about them.

_____

_____

_____

_____

_____

_____

_____

_____

_____

137. It is now becoming more common for children to begin to experiment sexually during their teens and some have also chosen this time to express their preference in same sex relationships. Many parents are caught off guard and struggle with these situations. Given this scenario in advance, how do you plan handle these issues with your child/children?

_____

_____

_____

_____

_____

_____

_____

_____

138. How would you manage the other children's' opinions or those or your family members if any of your children chose an alternative lifestyle?

_____

_____

_____

_____

_____

_____

_____

139. People seldom talk about or prepare themselves for the likelihood of a miscarriage, still birth, giving birth to children with physical challenges, health conditions, mental illnesses or other complications. Being unprepared makes it much more difficult and even takes its toll on all relationships involved. As a potential parent (if relevant), discuss this topic bringing to light any known conditions in your family history. Share your family medical history and health concerns and discuss how you would handle any of these scenarios.

_____

_____

_____

_____

_____

_____

_____

_____

_____

_____

_____

_____

_____

_____

_____

140. Children seem to be exposed to drugs and addictive substances earlier into their childhoods now. Some children succumb to peer pressure or develop a dependency on substances to deal with depression and other mental health issues. Share your experiences in this area and how you would proactively deal with substance abuse and the recreational use of drugs.

_____

_____

_____

_____

_____

_____

_____

_____

_____

_____

_____

_____

_____

_____

_____

_____

_____

_____

_____

141. Teenagers are plagued with emotional challenges that make their relationships with their parents extremely difficult. The statistics for runaway teens in the some countries are staggering. Not all make it back home safely. How will you or have you prepared yourselves as parents for these phases?

_____

_____

_____

_____

_____

_____

_____

_____

_____

_____

_____

_____

_____

_____

_____

_____

_____

_____

_____

Chapter Six

Past and Future Relationships

142. Describe any serious relationships you have had that lead to cohabitation, engagement or marriage.

_____

_____

_____

_____

_____

_____

_____

_____

_____

_____

143. How do you feel about possibly being in another long term relationship, engagement or marriage in the future?

_____

_____

_____

_____

_____

_____

_____

144. Do you enjoy being in a relationship? Why, or why not?

_____

_____

_____

_____

_____

_____

_____

145. On average, how much time do you tend to spend alone or single after a relationship? Please give your reasons.

_____

_____

_____

_____

_____

_____

146. In the past, what have you done, or accomplished during that time?

_____

_____

_____

_____

_____

_____

147. Do you date or see or other people immediately after a break up to help you get over it? If so, how do you believe rebound relationships help?

_____

_____

_____

_____

_____

_____

148. If you do engage in rebound relationships do you let the other person know your situation and the purpose of your relationship with them? If so, at which stage? If not, why not?

_____

_____

_____

_____

_____

149. Have you ever discovered that you were a part of a rebound relationship? Explain the events leading to your discovery and what happened next.

_____

_____

_____

_____

_____

_____

150. What do you enjoy most about being in a relationship?

_____

_____

_____

_____

_____

_____

_____

151. What past-times or activities do you enjoy in a relationship?

_____

_____

_____

_____

_____

_____

152. Describe your past romantic relationships. Identify the relationships you consider to have been significant and explain why these were significant to you.

_____

_____

_____

_____

_____

_____

The Significant Past - The Good

*The following questions should then be asked in turn for <u>each</u> **significant** relationship before moving on to the next relationship.*

153. In as far as you know did the other person also consider the relationship as being significant to them? If so, in what ways and if not, why not?

_____

_____

_____

_____

_____

_____

154. What level of commitment was reached in the relationship and how long did it last?

_____

_____

_____

_____

_____

_____

155. What are *your* best memories from this relationship?

_____

_____

_____

_____

_____

156. At which stages or occasions do **you** recall being your happiest?

_____

_____

_____

_____

_____

157. What had the other person done?

_____

_____

_____

_____

158. What had **you** done?

_____

_____

_____

_____

_____

159. How did this affect the way **you** viewed the other person?

_____

_____

_____

_____

_____

160. How did you being at your happiest affect the way **you** viewed the relationship and the effort you put into it?

_____

_____

_____

_____

161. How did it affect the way the other person viewed the relationship and the effort **they** put into it?

_____

_____

_____

_____

_____

162. Did you ever try, successfully or otherwise, intentionally or otherwise, to recreate this experience, even in another relationship and if so what was the outcome?

_____

_____

_____

_____

163. What did you learn from this?

_____

_____

_____

_____

_____

164. How did your happiest experiences affect **your** expectations from your future relationships/partners?

_____

_____

_____

_____

_____

165. In as far as you know, what were the other persons' best memories?

_____

_____

_____

_____

166. At which stages or occasions do you recall **them** being happiest?

_____

_____

_____

_____

167. What had **they** done?

_____

_____

_____

_____

_____

168. What had *you* done?

_____

_____

_____

_____

_____

169. How did your partners' happiness affect the way *they* viewed you?

_____

_____

_____

_____

_____

170. How did it affect the way *they* viewed the relationship and the effort *they* put into it?

_____

_____

_____

_____

_____

171. How did your partners' happiness affect the way *you* viewed the relationship and the effort *you* put into it?

_____

_____

_____

_____

172. Did you or they ever try, successfully or otherwise, intentionally or otherwise, to recreate this experience even in other relationships and if so what was the outcome?

_____

_____

_____

_____

_____

173. What did *you* learn from this?

_____

_____

_____

_____

_____

_____

174. How did your partners' happiness affect *your* expectations from your future relationships?

_____

_____

_____

_____

_____

_____

_____

The Significant Past - The Bad

*Now consider these questions for the same **significant** relationships*

175. What are **your** worst memories from your past relationships?

_____

_____

_____

_____

_____

_____

_____

_____

176. At which stages or occasions do **you** recall being saddest?

_____

_____

_____

_____

_____

_____

_____

177. What had the other person done?

_____

_____

_____

_____

_____

_____

_____

178. What had *you* done?

_____

_____

_____

_____

_____

_____

_____

179. How did *your* unhappiness affect the way *you* viewed the other person?

_____

_____

_____

_____

_____

_____

180. How did it affect the way *you* viewed the relationship and the effort *you* put into it?

_____

_____

_____

_____

_____

_____

181. How did your unhappiness affect the way your partner viewed the relationship and the effort *they* put into it?

_____

_____

_____

_____

_____

_____

_____

182. Did you or they ever try, successfully or otherwise, to intentionally or otherwise, recreate this experience, even in another relationship and if so what was the outcome?

_____

_____

_____

_____

_____

183. What did *you* learn from this?

_____

_____

_____

_____

_____

_____

_____

184. How did your unhappiness affect *your* expectations from *your* future relationships/partners?

_____

_____

_____

_____

_____

_____

185. In as far as you know, what were the other persons' worst memories?

_____

_____

_____

_____

_____

_____

186. At which stages or occasions do you recall them being *their* saddest?

_____

_____

_____

_____

_____

_____

187. What had *they* done?

_____

_____

_____

_____

_____

_____

188. What had *you* done?

_____

_____

_____

_____

_____

_____

_____

189. How did their unhappiness affect the way *they* viewed you?

_____

_____

_____

_____

_____

_____

_____

190. How did it affect the way *they* viewed the relationship and the effort *they* put into it?

_____

_____

_____

_____

_____

_____

191. How did their unhappiness affect the way *you* viewed the relationship and the effort *you* put into it?

_____

_____

_____

_____

_____

192. Did you or they ever try, successfully or otherwise, intentionally or otherwise, to recreate this experience again or in another relationship and if so what was the outcome?

_____

_____

_____

_____

_____

_____

193. What did *you* learn from this?

_____

_____

_____

_____

_____

_____

_____

_____

_____

194. How did your partners' unhappiness affect *your* expectations from your future relationships?

_____

_____

_____

_____

_____

_____

_____

_____

_____

_____

The Insignificant Past - The Good

*By this stage you should have reflected on the impact that both major and minor events had on the way you viewed your significant relationships. Now, describe the relationships you consider to have been **insignificant** by reflecting on the same questions for <u>each</u> individual relationship before moving on to the next relationship. The questions are guidelines, let the conversation flow freely*

195. In as far as you know did the other person also consider the relationship as being **insignificant** to them?

   _____

   _____

   _____

   _____

   _____

196. What level of commitment was reached in the relationship and how long did it last?

   _____

   _____

   _____

   _____

   _____

197. What are **your** best memories from this relationship?

   _____

   _____

   _____

   _____

198. At which stages or occasions do **you** recall being **your** happiest?

_____

_____

_____

_____

_____

_____

199. What had the other person done?

_____

_____

_____

_____

200. What had **you** done?

_____

_____

_____

_____

201. How did this affect the way **you** viewed the other person?

_____

_____

_____

_____

_____

202. How did you being at your happiest affect the way *you* viewed the relationship and the effort *you* put into it?

_____

_____

_____

_____

_____

203. How did it affect the way your partner viewed the relationship and the effort *they* put into it?

_____

_____

_____

_____

_____

204. Did you ever try, successfully or otherwise, intentionally or otherwise, to recreate this experience, even in another relationship and if so what was the outcome?

_____

_____

_____

_____

_____

205. What did *you* learn from this?

_____

_____

_____

206. How did your happiest experiences affect **your** expectations from **your** future relationships/partners?

_____

_____

_____

_____

_____

_____

207. In as far as you know, what were the other persons' best memories?

_____

_____

_____

_____

_____

208. At which stages or occasions do you recall **them** being happiest?

_____

_____

_____

_____

_____

209. What had **they** done?

_____

_____

_____

_____

210. What had *you* done?

_____

_____

_____

_____

_____

211. How did your partners' happiness affect the way *they* viewed you?

_____

_____

_____

_____

_____

212. How did it affect the way *they* viewed the relationship and the effort *they* put into it?

_____

_____

_____

_____

_____

213. How did your partners' happiness affect the way *you* viewed the relationship and the effort *you* put into it?

_____

_____

_____

_____

214. Did you or they ever try, successfully or otherwise, intentionally or otherwise, to recreate this experience even in other relationships and if so what was the outcome?

_____

_____

_____

_____

_____

215. What did *you* learn from this?

_____

_____

_____

_____

_____

_____

216. How did your partners' happiness affect **your** expectations from **your** future relationships?

_____

_____

_____

_____

_____

_____

_____

The Insignificant Past - The Bad

*Now consider these questions for the same **insignificant** relationships*

217. What are **your** worst memories from your past relationships?

_____

_____

_____

_____

_____

_____

_____

218. At which stages or occasions do you recall being saddest?

_____

_____

_____

_____

_____

_____

219. What had the other person done?

_____

_____

_____

_____

_____

_____

220. What had **you** done?

_____

_____

_____

_____

_____

_____

_____

221. How did **your** unhappiness affect the way **you** viewed the other person?

_____

_____

_____

_____

_____

_____

_____

222. How did it affect the way **you** viewed the relationship and the effort **you** put into it?

_____

_____

_____

_____

_____

_____

_____

223. How did your unhappiness affect the way your partner viewed the relationship and the effort **they** put into it?

_____

_____

_____

_____

_____

_____

_____

224. Did you or they ever try to, successfully or otherwise, intentionally or otherwise, recreate this experience, even in another relationship and if so what was the outcome?

_____

_____

_____

_____

_____

_____

225. What did you learn from this?

_____

_____

_____

_____

_____

_____

_____

226. How did your unhappiness affect **your** expectations from **your** future relationships/partners?

_____

_____

_____

_____

_____

_____

227. In as far as you know, what were the other persons' worst memories?

_____

_____

_____

_____

_____

_____

228. At which stages or occasions do you recall them being their saddest?

_____

_____

_____

_____

_____

_____

229. What had *they* done?

_____

_____

_____

_____

_____

230. What had *you* done?

_____

_____

_____

_____

_____

_____

_____

231. How did their unhappiness affect the way *they* viewed you?

_____

_____

_____

_____

_____

_____

_____

232. How did it affect the way **they** viewed the relationship and the effort **they** put into it?

_____

_____

_____

_____

_____

_____

233. How did their unhappiness affect the way **you** viewed the relationship and the effort **you** put into it?

_____

_____

_____

_____

_____

_____

_____

234. Did you or they ever try to, successfully or otherwise, intentionally or otherwise, recreate this experience again or in another relationship and if so what was the outcome?

_____

_____

_____

_____

_____

235. What did *you* learn from this?

_____

_____

_____

_____

_____

_____

_____

_____

_____

236. How did your partners' unhappiness affect *your* expectations from *your* future relationships?

_____

_____

_____

_____

_____

_____

_____

_____

_____

_____

Chapter Seven

More Introspection

237. In your current or future relationships what do you purpose to learn about the other person, both good and bad, and why is it important?

_____

_____

_____

_____

_____

_____

_____

_____

_____

_____

238. What have you *now* learnt about yourself, both good and bad from doing these exercises? What concerns do you now have, if any?

_____

_____

_____

_____

_____

_____

_____

239. Looking back over your early adulthood or dating experiences, how do you believe you have changed from all these experiences, if at all?

_____

_____

_____

_____

_____

_____

_____

_____

_____

_____

_____

240. Have you or others observed you behaving differently in your relationships and if so, in what ways?

_____

_____

_____

_____

_____

_____

_____

_____

241. Throughout your relationships in what ways have you become more or less of the following? Right now, is this book contributing in any way?

a. Cautious or fearful

_____

_____

_____

_____

_____

b. Trusting or open

_____

_____

_____

_____

_____

c. Intolerant or firm

_____

_____

_____

_____

_____

d. Forgiving or easy-going

_____

_____

_____

_____

e.   Independent or less dependent on a romantic partner

_____

_____

_____

_____

_____

f.   Spiritual or worldly

_____

_____

_____

_____

g.   Withdrawn or free

_____

_____

_____

_____

h.   Grateful or begrudging

_____

_____

_____

_____

_____

242. In what way do you believe or know your previous partners changed during and after their relationships with you?

_____

_____

_____

_____

_____

_____

_____

_____

_____

243. What have you ever tried to change anything about yourself or do differently to make a relationship work or to get another chance in a relationship? Tell your story.

_____

_____

_____

_____

_____

_____

_____

_____

_____

_____

244. If so, was it in an aspect or action previously indicated to you by your partner or something you thought to try? What were the results?

_____

_____

_____

_____

_____

_____

245. If the change brought about the intended result, did you continue with the change or not? Why or why not?

_____

_____

_____

_____

_____

_____

246. Did you ask the other person to make any concessions in exchange? If so, what were they? What was the result?

_____

_____

_____

_____

_____

_____

Chapter Eight

Financial Matters

Refer to the foundation laid out in the dating guide for this chapter

247. What are your main/major sources of income?

_____

_____

_____

_____

_____

_____

248. What are your auxiliary sources of income?

_____

_____

_____

_____

_____

_____

249. Please give details of the significant highs and lows of your financial history as well as major decisions/transactions that impacted you

_____

_____

_____

_____

_____

250. Do you believe your credit score is an accurate reflection of your financial history? Explain how you came to reach such a score?

_____

_____

_____

_____

_____

_____

_____

_____

_____

_____

251. If your financial history is used to gauge your level of financial responsibility, would you need to add any explanations to it? If so what would they be?

_____

_____

_____

_____

_____

_____

_____

_____

_____

252. Explain any debts you currently have. How long have you had these debts and how and why did you get into debt?

_____

_____

_____

_____

_____

_____

_____

253. How much is your debt and how do you plan to pay it off?

_____

_____

_____

_____

_____

254. Explain any financial assistance you have received or are receiving to help you pay your debts. Include anytime you considered or filed for bankruptcy.

_____

_____

_____

_____

_____

_____

_____

255. Have you filed all your tax returns for any/all countries in which you are required to do so? In which countries are you responsible for doing so and explain you filing status in each of these?

_____

_____

_____

_____

_____

_____

_____

_____

_____

256. Explain any arrears, liens, garnishments, student loans, or payment plans you have with any employer, agency, bank, and loan office, the IRS in the US or any government tax collection agency in any country.

_____

_____

_____

_____

_____

_____

_____

_____

_____

257. Do you owe taxes, loans, credit card debts, mortgages etc. from debts incurred from your previous relationships, marriage, businesses, family or children? Please explain extensively.

_____

_____

_____

_____

_____

_____

_____

_____

_____

258. Explain both your long-term and short-term major financial obligations.

_____

_____

_____

_____

_____

_____

_____

_____

_____

_____

259. Do you have expectations that your future spouse will help you clear or manage your debt or payments? Explain your answer and reasons.

_____

_____

_____

_____

_____

_____

260. Should your future spouse or partner fail to assist you what will that imply for your relationship or your future?

_____

_____

_____

_____

_____

261. Do you have any dependents? If so, whom and why?

_____

_____

_____

_____

_____

_____

262. Please explain if you have to pay child support or alimony to/for anyone

_____

_____

_____

_____

_____

_____

_____

263. Do you have or intend to take on any future student loans? Explain.

_____

_____

_____

_____

_____

_____

_____

264. Do you have a retirement plan that you have saved towards? Provide details please.

_____

_____

_____

_____

_____

_____

265. Do you have savings, a saving plan or how much are you able to set aside for savings every month?

_____

_____

_____

_____

_____

_____

_____

266. Are you currently saving up towards a purchase/investment? Explain.

_____

_____

_____

_____

_____

_____

_____

267. What percentage of your income goes towards your rent, car or other monthly payments if you have any of these financial commitments?

_____

_____

_____

_____

_____

268. If either parents or you or your partner needed/desired to live with you, how would you handle this? State your reasons please.

_____

_____

_____

_____

_____

_____

_____

_____

_____

_____

269. If it were a different family member would you handle this differently? How and why?

_____

_____

_____

_____

_____

_____

_____

_____

_____

_____

_____

270. Suppose a discussion with your partner revealed a family or cultural expectation requiring you both to be financially responsible for your parents and siblings, how would you proceed?

_____

_____

_____

_____

_____

_____

_____

_____

271. How would being a caretaker for your partners' family affect your commitment to the relationship?

_____

_____

_____

_____

_____

_____

_____

_____

272. Have you invested in any business projects, ventures, inventions, stocks, bonds or equity in the recent years? Please outline your Return on Investment (ROI) so far. Explain any other good/bad investments.

_____

_____

_____

_____

_____

_____

_____

_____

_____

273. Do you have any current investments or business ventures where you have partnered with a family member, friend or former spouse? Please explain the nature of the arrangement.

_____

_____

_____

_____

_____

_____

_____

_____

_____

_____

274. If you have you ever traded on the money market briefly describe your experiences.

_____

_____

_____

_____

_____

_____

275. Do you have a dream, ambition or goal that you would risk *everything* for? What is it and why do you feel it would be worth the risk?

_____

_____

_____

_____

_____

_____

276. Do you believe in consulting/involving your partner in all your major investment decisions? Explain your rationale.

_____

_____

_____

_____

_____

_____

277. What course of action would you take if there was no consensus on the way forward?

_____

_____

_____

_____

_____

_____

_____

278. Do you believe that one person in your relationship should have the final decision on financial matters? If so, who and how do you come that decision?

_____

_____

_____

_____

_____

279. Who have been your financial advisors in the past and to what extent do you still consult them or rely on their advice?

_____

_____

_____

_____

_____

_____

280. If you were suddenly out of work or without your sources of income, in order of importance, what would be your next steps?

_____

_____

_____

_____

_____

_____

_____

_____

_____

_____

_____

_____

_____

_____

_____

_____

_____

_____

Chapter Nine

Health, Sex and Intimacy

281. Describe your fitness or exercise routine if you have one. If not describe the level of physical activity you try to incorporate into your lifestyle.

_____

_____

_____

_____

_____

_____

_____

_____

_____

_____

282. Describe your physical, emotional and mental health history and present health and any awareness of current abnormalities or concerns.

_____

_____

_____

_____

_____

_____

_____

_____

283. Describe your family's history of illnesses.

_____

_____

_____

_____

_____

_____

_____

284. What is your personal or family history with sickness, allergies, surgeries and hospitalizations?

_____

_____

_____

_____

_____

_____

285. Are you aware of any chronic conditions that may be hereditary or that any of your family members may be prone to? Please give details.

_____

_____

_____

_____

_____

_____

286. Please explain any diagnoses you have received for any recent condition and the treatments you have had to undergo or are currently taking.

_____

_____

_____

_____

_____

_____

287. How do you cover your medical expenses, dental, health and vision included?

_____

_____

_____

_____

_____

_____

288. Do you have any upcoming costly medical treatments that you may have to finance partially or wholly? Please explain how you plan to do cover these costs.

_____

_____

_____

_____

_____

289. Would you consider going to the doctor as a couple to get tested? Please explain the reasons for your answer.

_____

_____

_____

_____

_____

_____

_____

290. When was your last dental, visual and annual physical/check-up?

_____

_____

_____

_____

_____

_____

291. Please explain the results including those for any lab work/ blood tests.

_____

_____

_____

_____

_____

_____

_____

Sexual Health

292. What is your understanding of the term "exclusive", when dating?

_____

_____

_____

_____

_____

_____

293. At what point in a dating relationship do you believe a couple should date exclusively? That is, stop dating or entertaining other suitors.

_____

_____

_____

_____

_____

_____

294. Do you usually assume the other person will feel the same way about being exclusive or do you take it upon yourself to communicate your expectations? What are your expectations?

_____

_____

_____

_____

_____

_____

295. If you do discuss the issue of being exclusive how do you bring it up?

_____

_____

_____

_____

_____

_____

296. How soon do you tend to find yourself sleeping with your partners?

_____

_____

_____

_____

_____

_____

297. How long would you *like* to wait, if at all, before being intimate with your partners? How do you tell them? Please explain why, why not?

_____

_____

_____

_____

_____

_____

298. Typically when does the conversation of ones' sexual history tend to come up; before or after you have engaged in a physical relationship with a partner or never? Please explain.

_____

_____

_____

_____

_____

_____

299. Do you feel in control of the physical aspect of your relationships or do you feel pressured to date the modern way? Please explain.

_____

_____

_____

_____

_____

_____

300. Do you often find yourself giving in to you or your partners' physical needs against your will? Please explain. Would you like this to change?

_____

_____

_____

_____

_____

_____

Sexually Transmitted Diseases and Infections

301. Describe any situations where you regretted being intimate with someone? Please explain

_____

_____

_____

_____

_____

_____

302. Did you talk to the person about it or discuss it with a friend, parent, counselor, pastor, aid worker etc. regarding this? Please explain.

_____

_____

_____

_____

_____

_____

303. Do you consider yourself as being sexually active? Please explain.

_____

_____

_____

_____

_____

_____

304. What methods of protection against pregnancy and sexually transmitted diseases/infections (STDs or STIs) do you use, if any?

_____

_____

_____

_____

_____

_____

_____

305. How did you decide who would be responsible for providing them?

_____

_____

_____

_____

_____

_____

306. How did the discussion come about? Who brought it up?

_____

_____

_____

_____

_____

_____

307. How do you feel about suggesting the use of protection? Does it make you uncomfortable? Do you fear it says something about you or what you think about the other person? Please explain what happens next.

_____

_____

_____

_____

_____

308. If you do use protection, do you prefer to wait for the other person to suggest it or do you take initiative and produce it when needed?

_____

_____

_____

_____

_____

309. Most couples stop using protection without any conversation about exclusivity, STD testing and alternate forms of protection. How, why and when do you stop using protection with your partner?

_____

_____

_____

_____

_____

310. It is not uncommon for both sexes to fear that they may offend the other party if they suggest protection. This is also the case where oral sex is concerned. Can you relate to this? Please share your thoughts on this?

_____

_____

_____

_____

_____

_____

311. How would you address this and if necessary reassure your partner?

_____

_____

_____

_____

_____

_____

312. Have you ever paid for sex, if so when and how often?

_____

_____

_____

_____

_____

313. If yes, do you still do so? If not, when and why did you stop?

_____

_____

_____

_____

_____

314. Have you ever been paid for sex or received gifts in exchange for sex?

_____

_____

_____

_____

_____

315. Does this still happen and if not, when did it stop and why?

_____

_____

_____

_____

_____

316. Have you ever contracted, been tested for *and* treated for any STIs or STD's? Which ones and when? Was the treatment successful?

_____

_____

_____

_____

317. If you have any sexually transmitted disease or infection that cannot be cured but can be managed with treatment, please explain.

_____

_____

_____

_____

_____

_____

318. If you are currently on any medications or regiments to suppress an outbreak or control the effects of any disease or condition not sexually transmitted, please explain.

_____

_____

_____

_____

_____

319. As far as you have been medically advised has anyone you have been recently seeing been exposed to any level of risk during? Should I be concerned? What do I need to tell my doctor?

_____

_____

_____

_____

_____

_____

320. How sure are you at present of all aspects of your health? What medical tests or assessments do you base that on?

_____

_____

_____

_____

_____

_____

321. Have you ever had to or chosen to disclose to someone that you had or still have an STI or STD? Please explain.

_____

_____

_____

_____

_____

322. Had you already been intimate with them and if so, had you suggested that they use protection, or had they done so? Was it used every time?

_____

_____

_____

_____

_____

323. If you had not yet been intimate with them please explain how the conversation arose and what happened next?

_____

_____

_____

_____

_____

_____

324. Has anyone ever suspected or even accused you of passing on an infection to them? Explain how you handled the situation and if you had been aware of having an infection or not.

_____

_____

_____

_____

_____

_____

325. Has anyone ever disclosed to you that *they* had an STI or STD? If so, at what stage did they advise you? What happened next?

_____

_____

_____

_____

_____

_____

_____

326. Had you already been intimate with them and if so, had either of you suggested or used protection every time? Who had suggested it?

_____

_____

_____

_____

_____

_____

327. What happened after this? Did you heed the warning and get tested?

_____

_____

_____

_____

_____

_____

328. Did you tell your other partners who might have been at risk? Explain

_____

_____

_____

_____

_____

_____

329. How many times have you been through this or similar experiences?

_____

_____

330. Have you ever found out, suspected or even accused someone of passing on an infection to you? Please explain the events.

_____

_____

_____

_____

_____

331. Did you confront them? Explain how they handled the situation and whether they had been aware of the risk or even suspicious.

_____

_____

_____

_____

_____

332. When you have been concerned that you had exposed yourself to some risk and later found out you were safe, did you make any changes to your sexual lifestyle? If yes, what were they and if no, why not?

_____

_____

_____

_____

Sexual Networks & Lifestyles

333. Describe your "sexual network/s" including any casual sex or "friends with benefits" arrangements you have had or still have.

_____

_____

_____

_____

_____

_____

_____

_____

_____

_____

_____

334. Are you still sexually involved with any former partners or parent/s of your child or children? Please explain.

_____

_____

_____

_____

_____

_____

_____

_____

_____

335. If you are or have been sexually active with your ex how often do you discuss exclusivity and use contraceptives to prevent unwanted pregnancies and sexually transmitted diseases and infections?

_____

_____

_____

_____

_____

_____

336. Have you ever had sexual relations with any persons of the same sex? If so, when and how often?

_____

_____

_____

_____

_____

_____

337. Did you asses your level of risk of contracting an STD/STI in same sex relations? How and what measures did/do you take?

_____

_____

_____

_____

_____

338. Have you ever participated in an orgy, group sex, swingers' groups or sex with strangers? If so, when and how often?

_____

_____

_____

_____

_____

_____

_____

339. Do you still have a preference for this nature of sexual activity with multiple partners or couples? Is this something you would like your future relationships to accommodate?

_____

_____

_____

_____

_____

340. Were you and your partners tested or using protection? If not what checks were set in place to ensure the risk was kept at a minimum?

_____

_____

_____

_____

_____

341. For how long and until when did you engage in this lifestyle?

_____

_____

_____

_____

_____

_____

342. Have you ever had sexual relations whilst under the influence of drugs, sedatives, alcohol, prescription medication or any mind altering substances? Explain.

_____

_____

_____

_____

_____

_____

343. Where you conscious all the time or fully aware of where you were or whom you were with and still willing to engage in these relations?

_____

_____

_____

_____

_____

_____

_____

Sexuality & Abuse

344. Are you comfortable with your physical appearance? If not, what would you like to change and why?

_____

_____

_____

_____

_____

_____

345. Do you consider yourself to be sexually attractive? Explain.

_____

_____

_____

_____

_____

_____

346. As a child/youth did you ever fantasize about being the opposite sex or did you dress in the opposite sex' clothes? Please explain.

_____

_____

_____

_____

_____

_____

_____

_____

347. As a child/youth did you fantasize about being intimate with the same sex? Please explain.

_____

_____

_____

_____

_____

_____

_____

348. Did your fantasies stop? Please explain how and when?

_____

_____

_____

_____

_____

If they did not stop, did you ever consider, talk about or pursue a trans-gender, trans-sexual or homosexual lifestyle? Please explain.

_____

_____

_____

_____

_____

_____

349. Did you or would you like to undergo a sex change or gender reassigning operation or cross dress? Please explain.

_____

_____

_____

_____

_____

_____

_____

_____

350. Have you ever been forced to have relations with anyone against your will? If you are comfortable discussing the situation, please explain what happened in all the incidents you are referring to.

_____

_____

_____

_____

_____

_____

_____

_____

_____

_____

_____

_____

351. Have you ever been forced to have relations with anyone of the *same* sex/gender against your will? If you are comfortable discussing the situation, please explain what happened in all the incidents you are referring to.

_____

_____

_____

_____

_____

352. Have you ever been the victim of sexual abuse, rape, sexual assault, date rape or any other unwanted sexual aggression? Please explain.

_____

_____

_____

_____

_____

_____

353. Were you married, or in a committed relationship at the time? Did you tell your partner what happened? Explain.

_____

_____

_____

_____

354. If the aggressor was someone other than the person you were involved with did you tell them? Please give your reasons.

_____

_____

_____

_____

_____

_____

_____

355. If the aggressor was your partner or someone you were dating at the time did you continue to stay in the relationship or see them? Why?

_____

_____

_____

_____

_____

_____

_____

356. Did you report the incident, seek counselling and get tested? Explain.

_____

_____

_____

_____

_____

357. Is watching or reading pornography a part of your former or current lifestyle? Please explain to what extent.

_____

_____

_____

_____

_____

_____

358. Do you keep pornographic material around the house/office, on your computer or phone, or do you just access it when you need it? Explain.

_____

_____

_____

_____

_____

_____

359. Do you call sex hotlines or engage in internet sex chat rooms? How often do you do so and for how long have you been doing this?

_____

_____

_____

_____

_____

_____

360. Have you ever been suspected or caught cheating, or voluntarily confessed to doing so? Explain how this situation arose and ended.

_____

_____

_____

_____

_____

_____

_____

_____

361. Have you ever been cheated on? Explain the circumstances and how you discovered this. What did you do about it if anything?

_____

_____

_____

_____

_____

_____

_____

_____

_____

_____

_____

362. Do you know if protection was used during the affair/s or infidelity?

_____

_____

_____

_____

_____

_____

363. If you have been unfaithful more than once, please explain if this was with different people each time and the nature of your relationships.

_____

_____

_____

_____

_____

_____

_____

364. Have *you* ever been accused of being unfaithful? Explain how the accusation came about and if there really was an affair?

_____

_____

_____

_____

_____

365. Did any of your relationships end because of infidelity? Please explain.

_____

_____

_____

_____

_____

366. Did any pregnancies arise from sexual relations outside of your relationship? Was/is there a paternity dispute in any of these? Explain.

_____

_____

_____

_____

_____

367. Were any children subsequently born? What is your relationship to them?

_____

_____

_____

_____

368. Were any of these pregnancies terminated? Explain why, if you know.

_____

_____

_____

369. Did you and any of your former partners ever conceive, and if so, were any pregnancies terminated or result in a miscarriage? Explain

_____

_____

_____

_____

_____

_____

_____

370. How did any pregnancy affect you and your relationship?

_____

_____

_____

_____

_____

_____

371. How did the loss of any pregnancies affect you and your relationship?

_____

_____

_____

_____

_____

_____

372. As far as you know, did the termination of any pregnancies affect your ability or desire to have children? How?

_____

_____

_____

_____

_____

_____

_____

373. What measures or recourse did you take to improve or ensure your chances of having children in the future?

_____

_____

_____

_____

_____

374. Do your family and friends know about what you went through and are they willing to be your support group in the event that you experience this again?

_____

_____

_____

_____

_____

Chapter Ten

Religion and Faith

360. How would you define your faith or describe your spiritual life?

_____

_____

_____

_____

_____

_____

_____

361. Were you raised in a home, school or place of worship that practiced tithing, offering and giving of alms or sacrifices? Please explain.

_____

_____

_____

_____

_____

362. What are your views on tithing (giving a tenth of your income)?

_____

_____

_____

_____

363. Do you tithe, and if so, what percent of your income, or how do you arrive at your amount?

_____ _____

_____

_____

_____

_____

364. If you do not tithe, why not?

_____

_____

_____

_____

365. Would you be agreeable to your spouse also tithing if you are tithing too? Explain.

_____

_____

_____

_____

_____

366. If so, what percent would you find to be agreeable for them to tithe?

_____

_____

_____

_____

367. What other monetary and non-monetary contributions or donations do you make to houses of faith or religious ministries?

_____

_____

_____

_____

_____

_____

368. What are your views on volunteering in such places?

_____

_____

_____

_____

_____

_____

369. Where you raised in a home, school or place of worship that taught prayer? Describe your experiences.

_____

_____

_____

_____

_____

_____

_____

370. Describe your regular prayer or meditation routine.

_____

_____

_____

_____

_____

_____

_____

371. What are your views on praying together as a couple?

_____

_____

_____

_____

_____

_____

372. If fasting (abstaining from eating) is a part of your prayer lifestyle, please explain your experiences with it and how you go about it.

_____

_____

_____

_____

_____

_____

_____

373. What are your views on sexual activities between couples when fasting? Explain how strongly you may or may not feel about this.

_____

_____

_____

_____

_____

_____

374. How do you determine which matters to pray about and leave to God and which ones to handle on your own?

_____

_____

_____

_____

_____

_____

375. Should you and your partner not agree on this who do you believe should make the final determination? How and why?

_____

_____

_____

_____

_____

_____

_____

376. What do you believe is the spiritual role of the husband in a marriage? What does this mean to you?

_____

_____

_____

_____

_____

_____

_____

_____

_____

_____

377. What do you believe is the spiritual role of the wife in a marriage? What does this mean to you?

_____

_____

_____

_____

_____

_____

_____

_____

_____

378. Describe the spiritual or religious lifestyle you desire to have with your future family. Where do you get your ideals from?

_____

_____

_____

_____

_____

_____

_____

_____

_____

379. Where you raised in a home, school or place of worship that taught the reading of religious literature or writings? How did this influence you?

_____

_____

_____

_____

_____

_____

_____

_____

_____

_____

_____

380. Describe the different religions or spiritual practices you have studied, witnessed, participated in or actively engaged in.

_____

_____

_____

_____

_____

_____

_____

_____

381. Describe your experiences with superstition.

_____

_____

_____

_____

_____

382. Explain your perspective and experiences with astrology, numerology and other forms of divination.

_____

_____

_____

_____

_____

_____

383. Explain your beliefs on the devil, demons, ghosts, evil powers, evil presences, curses, possession, witchcraft etc. Describe any experiences you may have had with any of these.

_____

_____

_____

_____

_____

_____

_____

_____

_____

_____

384. Describe any experiences you may have had with psychics, clairvoyants, tarot card readers, fortune tellers etc.

_____

_____

_____

_____

_____

_____

_____

_____

_____

_____

_____

385. Describe any experiences you may have had with any seers, prophets or any prophecies given to you. Describe their impact on your life.

_____

_____

_____

_____

_____

_____

386. Would you consider a vocation as a spiritual leader, prophet, rabbi, minister, pastor or priest, or whichever title is relevant in your faith/religion? Give your reasons.

_____

_____

_____

_____

_____

387. If your partner was considering any of these vocations what would your position be?

_____

_____

_____

_____

_____

388. If your child was considering such a vocation what would your position on this be?

_____

_____

_____

_____

_____

_____

_____

389. What role would you like your spiritual leaders to have in your marital/spouse relationship, if any?

_____

_____

_____

_____

_____

_____

390. If you or your partner have ever been spiritual leaders, recount the details and state your expectations for doing so again in the future.

_____

_____

_____

_____

_____

_____

391. What role would you like your family members or parents to have in your marital/spouse relationship, if any?

_____

_____

_____

_____

_____

_____

392. Have you ever been actively involved in a couples' marriage? Recount the details and state your expectations for doing so again in the future. .

_____

_____

_____

_____

_____

_____

393. Would you ever seriously consider spiritual marital/spousal counseling for the sake of saving *your* relationship? Give your reasons.

_____

_____

_____

_____

_____

_____

394. Explain your thoughts on couples' therapy, counselling and marriage seminars?

_____

_____

_____

_____

_____

_____

_____

_____

_____

395. Would you ever seriously consider spiritual marital/spousal counseling for the sake of your own personal development if recommended?

_____

_____

_____

_____

_____

_____

_____

_____

_____

_____

Finally, as you discover and digest all sorts of thoughts whilst reading this book please take the time to connect me on the blog. Go to http://wwww.doaskdotellbooks.com and let me know …

396. Was this book helpful to you? Please explain.

_____

_____

_____

_____

_____

_____

397. What issues or questions would you have liked to see addressed?

_____

_____

_____

_____

_____

398. If you feel better equipped to handle relationships, please share how.

_____

_____

_____

_____

_____

_____

399. Did this book help you get out of a relationship you didn't need to be in? Explain.

_____

_____

_____

_____

_____

_____

_____

_____

_____

400. Did this book help your relationship or marriage? Please share how.

_____

_____

_____

_____

_____

_____

_____

_____

_____

Chapter Eleven

Embrace the Change

Remember that ideally, in marriage and long term commitments or relationships, couples should strive to not take each other for granted. Everyone changes over time. Just as our taste in clothes, food, drink, places, social groups, friends and even churches change over time, we must allow for the special people in our lives to also evolve. Let us allow them to grow into new preferences and not hold them hostage to who they were when we met them.

So many couples fail to keep up with or even simply accommodate each other's' growth. They feel cheated and would rather end the relationship than embrace change and accept that even *they* too have changed and that it isn't always a bad thing. Just as preferences change several times during a lifetime so does the direction we take in many areas of our lives.

All people change gradually or rapidly but we can eliminate the chances of discovering this in an unpleasant way. We can do so by asking timely, pertinent questions and being in the right mind-set to embrace the change.

Reflect on what you both have shared and then allow yourselves to be in awe of each other. Acknowledge each other for dealing with the past or even overcoming despair, heartaches, heartbreaks, abuse, derailment of dreams and ambitions and all sorts of challenges.

Then what if after all this one of you chooses to leave the relationship? Let them. Consider the possibility of staying in a relationship which you now know is not right for you. How can you truly commit? You could take your dissatisfaction out on the other person because you expect them to **make** you happy in return for staying. That is a great burden to place on any being.

Discuss your concerns and realize that if you choose to leave the relationship based on what you have learnt it's about **you** not the other person. It is YOU and not them that have the issue. They may be able to live with all this whereas you may not be able to. That does not make either of you bad people.

So avoid making them feel responsible for your choice to end it, if you do. If they choose to end the relationship, try not to see it as a punishment for your past. Try to accept that they had the right to choose whether they can or cannot handle the truth.

Your Partner is a Survivor, Celebrate Them!

Remember, life may have been cruel to your partner so avoid causing more hurt by being insensitive, judgmental, interrogating them, being mean, hurtful, , cynical or untrustworthy; just because you can't handle their truth.

So what if in your quest for a stronger bond you;

- You find some uncomfortable truths? Embrace them.

- What if you feel cheated? Forgive.

- Overwhelmed and confused? Pray. Meditate.

If after all this you cannot live with the entirety of your loved ones' past, present and future then admit it. It's **your** failure to accept their truth, not theirs to meet your expectations. Then be a person of honor and keep their secrets till your death, but all the while celebrating *them*.

For every day you and your loved one open your eyes to a brand new dawn, you must celebrate surviving your yesterdays and your yester nights. If you or they are here today, well say a prayer, sing a song, pop a cork, blow up some balloons, turn up the radio, do a jive and do what you have to do to get your celebration spirit in gear!

You have both survived everything that life has hurled at you from the womb till today!

A good book to read if the thought of being alone daunts you is *Married, Single and Divorced* by Dr. Myles Munroe. This book allows your mind to stroll down other corridors that show the amazing possibilities of your life ahead.

I also strongly recommend his teachings on the *Benefits on Being Single*. This book gives a diverse selection of things that single people have the advantage to do. You may definitely have time to do them now; travelling, learning a foreign language, supporting parents, taking a course, the list only opens up your mind to more.

Celebrate your singleness. Merely enduring it until you find another relationship is to short change yourself of a great stage to rest your mind, values, finances etc.

Chapter Twelve

Conclusion

At best, the thought of unearthing all the history and experiences that have shaped and defined both your lives, values, principles and ambitions may seem daunting at this stage. Then perhaps the realization that there may be some unpleasant truths behind the questions that you both need to have answered may have given you sleepless nights.

Eventually the fear of facing and embracing the hidden truths beneath the questions may seem more hazardous to the relationship than the seeming reality of what you have. You could just read this book and wonder about what you don't know. Or you could seek to understand yourself and appreciate your partner better in the light of what you both have survived?

If your fear of the unknown and your fear of rocking this boat still overwhelm you, consider this, that the end of **every** love relationship is painful. Be it that the other person chooses to end the relationship unexpectedly, or it ends before one of you is willing to give up; or because the absence endured in a long distance relationship has taken its toll, or the feelings have changed or the other has died.

Any action that signals the summarily end of a relationship results in some pain or disappointment for at least one of you.

Yet knowing this full well, we still embark on the journey of love. We fully embrace the opportunity to grow in significance and vulnerability in another persons' life. We do so without weighing the imminent joys against the inevitable pain at the end of it all. Why?

The good times and memories make the bad times worth it. When we see how we become better in some ways when we are in love we constantly yearn for it. We start to dream bigger, work harder, write poetry, become romantic, care for another, enjoy human touch, and simply live wholly. Until it ends.

Bitter sweet memories and tears are shared but we wouldn't change much for the opportunity to have given our best and loved beyond our previous capacity. We recover from the pain only to become sentimental, try harder than the last relationship, become even more sentimental and forgive without keeping count; all because we felt honored that love has chosen us and found us. Again.

For Better or Worse!

If, however, you both choose to stay, and make a better relationship out of your union then do so while celebrating each other. Celebrate your partner, their ability to share all this with you. Celebrate *your* ability to trust, perhaps, again. Fully embrace the new fold opportunity to see more value and worth in your loved one and even in yourself.

For the married folks, do not be afraid to ask for help or to admit you are struggling. Your success will be sweeter when you make it. Get counseling. More people do than you may think. Confide in your pastors or spiritual elders. Find a couple that you both love and respect to guide you through any difficult phases.

Trust God to heal the past. Then use it only as a reference point to encourage yourself and motivate others. Trust God to place the right people in your present, because He alone knows your future. Then don't wait a **whole long year** to celebrate your anniversary, your existence, your love. Pick random days in the year to celebrate and appreciate each other.

Finally, when you have found your life partner and have weathered some storms and have awesome stories to share, go mentor and guide some young people. This old fashioned yet revolutionary way of dating works. Start them early on this path so that they can see how their present lifestyles may have consequences in the future.

Open up your relationship to them without violating each other's trust. Show them how to grow in love and how to forgive even when it isn't easy. Show them how some things need not be surprises in life. Give the gift of this book and workbook and spread the love.

How dare anyone hold anything

against those whom God has

forgiven?

Remember to forgive yourself,

Lest you are found to be in

contempt

Of not forgiving someone He

died for!

© 2015

But if in all time one could convince me

That to be loved is but the most exciting

Passion to feel in all the earth,

I can, and must do far better

To make them believe,

That to love, exceeds all else

In its totality.

To love unreservedly

And to give of oneself

Without thought at all times...

Tis freedom indeed

© 1993

Also available by this author:

DO ASK, DO TELL

A ROMANTIC REVOLUTION

DATING GUIDE

BY

CHRISTINA CHEMHURU (M.B.A.)

FORWARD BY

DR. MYLES MUNROE

Proof

Made in the USA
Charleston, SC
07 August 2015